Table of contents

CW01499582

Other Books by Rita Faith

Neville Goddard: Master Your Inner Game to Achieve Your Every Desire – Book 1 Inner Talking

Mastering Your Inner World Neville Goddard Explained – Manifesting with Ease

"The only acceptable gift is a joyful heart. Come with singing and praise. That is the way to come before the Lord – your own consciousness. "

"Assume the feeling of your wish fulfilled, and you have brought the only acceptable gift. All states of mind other than that of the wish fulfilled are an abomination; they are superstition and mean nothing." – Neville Goddard

Introduction

In this book I introduce with my own interpretation and insights, two rare radio talks and three lectures from Neville Goddard whom I believe to be one of the greatest teachers on spiritual and mystic matters. A true genius in the realm of reality creation and manifesting.

Each chapter is preceded with my introduction and advice on the material that is then presented by Neville. He taught with such authority as he had experienced the truth of his own teachings, he believed in them as he had lived them. I have also experienced the truth of his teachings and it is my desire that you do too. This is the reason behind the creation of this book. This book contains spiritual truths. I believe everyone deserves to know these truths, to experience this power the power to create your very own heaven on earth.

I spent numerous months selecting from the hundreds of Neville's lectures and talks, the five that I believe will truly change your life and also help you to become the master of your fate. If I can do it you can do it to.

Let me give you a little background on who I am and a glimpse into my past and present life. I was born into a borderline poverty stricken catholic family the middle child in a family of three. I spent my childhood growing up in a family, where domestic violence was the norm. I always felt like a misfit, never quite fitting in. I felt weird and different, even from an early age I was searching for something. I just didn't know what that was.

I couldn't accept the catholic religion, even although I tried. The teaching always felt off to me, but it still managed to affect me, the feelings of unworthiness that grew from being taught that I was born clothed in sin and therefore inherently I was somehow bad.

My childhood was turbulent and confusing. I was abused at the age of eleven, fortunately at this age it wasn't an ongoing situation of abuse and was an isolated event. It affected me profoundly and I turned inward and isolated myself, this was my way of coping with what had happened.

Fast forward to my middle teenage years and I had experienced attempted abuse on several occasions. My feelings of unworthiness grew although I did an excellent job of hiding this and pushing my emotions and feelings deep inside. However I believed that there must be something wrong with me, that I must be bad, it must be my fault I was to blame in some way.

I struggled for years from my late teens all the way into adulthood with depression and anxiety. I still felt different from others, I thought myself weird. I joined a cult searching for meaning, searching for God, searching for myself. I didn't find it with the cult, although I did give the cult most of my money in an attempt to find what I was seeking. I found nothing but an increased feeling of despair and unworthiness. After a few years I left the cult. Tried to forget about finding God, tried to put my search to an end and accept that maybe this was all there is.

My life turned into a series of fortunate and unfortunate events and circumstances, a cycle of some happiness then sadness, disappointments, struggle and lack. Until I couldn't take it anymore and I again began my search. My search led me to Jane Roberts and the Seth material. I devoured all the books. I remember the first time I read the Seth book the Nature of Personal Reality, my mind boggled but there was movement within me, a feeling that it was true on some level. For the first time I realized that my feelings of despair and the belief in my own unworthiness were manifesting in my life as events and circumstances.

I continued on my path for spiritual knowledge and truth and have over the years researched and studied an enormous amount of books and material from many of the great spiritual masters and mystics of our time. However I still continued searching. I was gaining considerable knowledge but it was only knowledge. I was not living the knowledge. I would apply some of the techniques and principles, I also got some success but it wasn't consistent. I was continually reacting to events and circumstances, trying to change things, trying to force things. In short I was working against myself I was trying to change my circumstances in desperation and in frustration and so nothing was changing and in many areas my life got worse. That all changed when I found Neville Goddard or as I like to think Neville found me.

Why am I telling you all this? Because if you have been studying this for years and not getting the results and changes you desire, I want you to know that I have been there I know what it is like, I know how you feel and I want to show you that you do have the power to change your life and these teachings will help you do that.

Failure is either the result of; gaining the knowledge but not applying it consistently; working against yourself through your feelings; applying too much effort trying to force change in desperation; focusing on the "how" and not living in the end; not walking and acting in the conviction that your wish is fulfilled; feeling unworthy; feeling like a victim; not truly believing that your imagination is God.

Finally not taking responsibility for every circumstance, event and ultimately everything and everyone in your life. If you don't accept full responsibility you will continue on some level to feel like a victim and there is no power in victimhood. If you really believe you are a victim of events, circumstances or people, you are playing the part of a victim, and you will attract situations and people that will confirm the reality of the part you are playing, that of victim. We are all playing parts in this great drama of life, which part you play is entirely your own choosing.

"No man cometh unto me save I call him. You didn't choose me; I have chosen you. No man can take away my life; I lay it down myself. There is no power to take from me anything that is part of the inner arrangement of my mind." – Neville Goddard

You are the operant power of your imagination, you have the gift, a true gift of imagination and the free will to choose what you will focus on, the feelings that you allow to entertain. The choice of how you will react in any situation. You can change your life. Are you ready to accept this?

Neville Goddard's teachings changed my life. I have gone from working in a job I hated, to working for myself from my home on my own terms doing something that I love. I have transformed my relationships. I have gone from living paycheck to paycheck to always having more than enough. I have travelled to most parts of the World. I have gone from depression and anxiety to happiness and peace.

You can do this too. The teachings in this book are profound and if you read with an open mind and actually apply the teachings to every area in your daily life you will change your World. This isn't about a quick fix or to put a patch on circumstances you don't want or like. It's a lifestyle, it's a way of life and if you live by these teachings and I mean really live them you will experience these truths.

You will experience God in You. You will create your very own Heaven on Earth.

Enjoy the journey, be excited. I wish you every success in the World.

Seeing Through the Eye of God

In this chapter Neville talks about the power of feeling in his 1951 radio talk; Feeling is the Secret. Feelings are the turbo charge in manifestation, the importance of which cannot be over looked. It doesn't matter what you think about if you don't charge the thoughts with the appropriate feeling, they are wasted thoughts or worse if you are thinking thoughts of abundance but at the same time feeling desperation, the thoughts of abundance will not manifest, what will manifest is more desperation, in the form of events and circumstances. This is why so many people experience failure with their attempts to manifest more money, love, health or happiness. The thoughts do not match the feeling within us and it is our feelings which manifest, always keep this thought in your awareness when you are manifesting.

Neville explains that we say we are happy because we are well, we assume being well is the cause of our happiness in our outer world, not realizing that, our feelings of happiness also create the conditions of wellness, this can also be related to Joseph's Murphy's Law of Inverse Transformation which basically means that if a physical fact can produce a certain psychological state, then in reverse a psychological state can produce a physical fact. In other words if an event or circumstances can trigger certain emotional states, then those emotional states can be used to create desired events and circumstances. Therefore to live in the feelings of wealth, wealth will be produced in our physical world and so on. It is not the outer world that creates our feelings, but our feelings which create our outer world. The inner leads the outer. The state sought must be felt and lived in before its physical manifestation; this is what brings it into form.

If we did nothing else but feel good and feel loving and well and joyous, our world would literally transform itself, we would have changed our emotional pattern, and this new emotional pattern would be reflected back to us in our outer world. When you are imagining with feeling you are effectively praying, and when you pray like this and remain faithful to that feeling you are giving thanks for its manifestation, this is believing that you have received. This is total surrender to the feeling of the wish fulfilled and it will objectify itself in your reality. There is nothing more important than feeling, without feeling there is no power.

This is Imaginative Love, if you would ignore reason and the evidence of your senses and contemplate and feel only the ideals you wish to see realized, as if they were a present fact you are literally seeing through the Eye of God. Seeing and feeling everything as perfect. Judge not, whatever you wish and think true of another, you are effectively wishing for yourself. You cannot escape the results of your reactions to life. Seeing through the Eye of God you only imagine others as you desire them to be, you see them through love and imagine with feeling only the best for them and yourself. Then watch as your World transforms itself.

This rare radio talk will transform your way of thinking and ultimately your life, read and re-read it so that the information goes deep into your mind, if you did nothing else but truly grasp what Neville is teaching here, and apply it faithfully you will transform your life!

Feeling Is the Secret

Radio Talk, Station KECA, Los Angeles, (July, 1951)

Recently, I asked a very successful businessman his formula for success. He laughed and was a little embarrassed. Then he replied. "I guess it's just because I can't conceive of failure. It's nothing that I think about much. It's more a feeling that I have"

His statement coincided completely with my own beliefs and experiments. We can think about something forever and never see it in our world, but once let us feel its reality, and we are bound to encounter it. The more intensely we feel, the sooner we will encounter it.

We all regard feelings far too much as effects, and not sufficiently as causes of the events of the day. Feeling is not only the result of our conditions of life; it is also the creator of those conditions. We say we are happy because we are well, not realizing that the process will work equally well in the reverse direction. We are well because we are happy. We are all far too undisciplined in our feelings.

To be joyful for another is to bless ourselves as well as him. To be angry with another is to punish ourselves for his fault. The distressed mind stays at home though the body travels to the ends of the earth, while the happy mind travels though the body remains at home.

Feeling is the secret of successful prayer, for in prayer, we feel ourselves into the situation of the answered prayer and, then, we live and act upon that conviction. Feeling after Him, as the Bible suggests, is a gradual unfolding of the soul's hidden capacities. Feeling yields in importance to no other. It is the ferment without which no creation is possible. All forms of creative imagination imply elements of feeling. All emotional dispositions whatever may influence the creative imagination. Feeling after Him has no finality. It is an acquisition, increasing in proportion to receptivity, which has not and never will have finality.

An idea which is only an idea produces nothing and does nothing. It acts only if it is felt, if it is accompanied by effective feeling. Somewhere within the soul there is a mood which, if found, means wealth, health, happiness to us. The creative desire is innate in man. His whole happiness is involved in the impulse to create.

Because men do not perfectly "feel" the results of their prayers they are unsure, when they might be perfectly sure. We read Proverbs, "A merry heart doeth good like a medicine but a broken spirit drieth the bones." Orchestral hearts burn in the oil of the lamp of the king. The spirt sings unto the Lord a new song. All true prayer wears a glad countenance; the good are anointed with the oil of gladness above their fellows.

Let us then, watch our feelings, our reactions to the day's events. And let us guard our feelings even more zealously in the act of prayer, for prayer is the true creative state. Dignity indicates that man hears the greater music of life, and moves to the tempo of its deeper meaning. If we did nothing but imagine and feel the lovely, the world's reform would, at once, be accomplished. Many of the stories of the Bible deal exclusively with the power of imagination and feeling.

"Feeling after Him" is the cry of the truth seeker. Only imagination and feeling can restore the Eden from which experience has driven us. Feeling and imagination are the senses by which we perceive the beyond. Where knowledge ends, they begin. Every noble feeling of man is the opening for him of some door to the divine world. Let us measure men, not by the height of their cities, but by the magnificence of their imaginations and feelings. Let us turn our thought up to Heaven and mix our imagination with the angels. The world that moves us is the one we imagine, not the world that surrounds us. In the imagination lie the unexplored continents, and man's great future adventure.

This consciousness of non-finality in "feeling after God" has been the experience of all earnest God-ward feelers. They realize that their conception of the Infinite has constantly deepened and expanded with experience. Those who endeavour to think out the meaning of the experience and to coordinate it with the rest of our knowledge are the philosophic mystics; those who try to develop the faculty in themselves and to deepen the experience are the practical or experimental mystics.

Some, and among them the greatest, have tried to do both. Religion begins in subjective experience. Religion is what a man does with his solitude, for in solitude we are compelled to subjective experience.

God never changes; it is we who are changing; our spiritual eyes are ever getting keener; and this enlargement of truth will bring us an ever-increasing inner peace.

The best defence against the deceptive assault upon our mental and moral eyesight is the spiritual eye or the Eye of God. In other words, a spiritual ideal that cannot be changed by circumstance, a code of personal honor and integrity in ourselves and good will and love to others. "Not what thou art, nor what thou hast been, beholdeth God with his merciful eyes, but that thou wouldst be."

Through the veins of the humblest man on earth runs royal blood of being. Therefore, let us look at man through the eyes of imaginative love which is really seeing with the Eye of God. Under the influence of the Eye of God, the ideal rises up out of the actual as water is etherialized by the sun into the imagery cloudland. Things altogether distant are present to the spiritual eye.

The Eye of God makes the future dream a present fact. Not four months to harvest – look again, if we persist in this seeing, one day we will arise with the distance in our eyes, and all the staying, stagnant nearby will suddenly be of no importance. We will brush it aside as we pass on to our far-seen objective.

The man who really finds himself cannot do otherwise than let himself be guided by love. He is of too pure eyes to behold iniquity. Our ability to help others will be in proportion to our ability to control and help ourselves. The day a man achieves victory over himself, history will discover that to have been a victory over his enemy. The healing touch is in an attitude, and one day man will discover that one governs souls only with serenity. The mighty surrenders itself fully only to the most gentle.

Recognizing the power of feeling, let us pay strict attention to our moods and attitudes. Every stage of man's progress is made through the exercise of his imagination and feeling. By creating an "ideal" within our mental sphere we can feel ourselves into this "ideal image" till we become one and the same with it, absorbing its qualities into the very core of our being. The solitary or captive can, by the intensity of his imagination and feeling, effect myriads so that he can act through many men and speak through many voices. Extend your feelers, trust your touch, participate in all flights of your imaginations and be not afraid of your own sensitivities.

The best way to feel another's good is to be more intensely aware of it. Be like my friend and have "more of a feeling" for the health, the wealth, the happiness you desire. Ideas do not bless unless they descend from Heaven and take flesh. Make your results or accomplishments the crucial test of true imagination.

As you observe these results, you will determine to fill your images with love and walk in a high and noble mood for you will know with the poet:

"That which ye sow ye reap.

See yonder fields

The sesamum was sesamum, the corn

Was corn. The Silence and the Darkness knew

So is man's fate born."

True Meditation

Meditation can be daunting for anyone when first starting the process of integrating it into daily life. I remember when I first started out practicing meditation I would become frustrated and annoyed with myself because I could not silence my mind, no matter how hard I tried I could not achieve no thought and I assumed that I was a failure at meditation, to the point that at one stage of my life I gave up on meditation altogether. It became a chore that only led to me feeling frustrated.

That all changed when I came across the following radio talk from Neville, which explains beautifully what meditation actually is and how to practice and use meditation to successfully manifest desires. I realized that my own failure with meditation was caused by too much effort and trying to clear my mind of all thought. Therefore I was not giving any idea to my consciousness that would allow for the effortless holding of my attention on an idea or a desire to feed on and become absorbed in the feeling of fulfilment.

Meditation is actually surrendering to the feeling of the wish fulfilled. Simply put meditation is a controlled imagination, a steadying of attention on an idea or desire combined with the feeling that it is accomplished. So that this idea and feeling are completely absorbed into your consciousness; to such an extent that it crowds out all other thoughts and feelings.

It is the power of attention solely fixed on the desirable, the state sought and becoming immersed in it, with such depth of feeling that nothing else can penetrate it. Rather that no thought and complete silence of the mind, it is the control of attention and imagination with least effort, lovingly placed and contemplated in your imagination like a seed and using the power of your feeling to ensure that the seed goes deep into the fertile soil of your mind and watered with attention to the feeling of the wish fulfilled, so that your seed will grow into the most bountiful harvest in your outer world.

It is important to hold your attention solely on the idea or desire you wish to see realized this is the difference between success and failure. If your attention wanders in any way, gently bring it back to the desire and the feeling of fulfilment, and do so over and over again, until you become so absorbed into it, that your attention effortlessly holds the thought and feeling of accomplishment. It takes on all the tones of reality, in other words what you are experiencing in imagination, feels real.

If we fail to persistently bring our attention back to the fulfilment and feeling of our desire, we will find that we have allowed our thought and feeling to have been lured away down many different avenues, far removed from the idea we wished to realize.

Meditation is nothing more than a relaxed state, where we shut out the outside world, our reason and the evidence of the senses and go within, to experience in imagination what we wish to experience in our outer world. This can be done anywhere and from any length of time, from a few minutes to upward of an hour if you so desire. All it is, is absorption into an idea and the feeling of its fulfilment. It is a complete surrender while holding the attention, firmly on the desire to be realized.

Mediation then becomes a joy and you will so relish the time you spend in this state of pure relaxed imagination. I hope the following words of Neville; speak to you the way they spoke to me.

Meditation

Radio Talk, Station KECA, Los Angeles (July, 1951)

Many people tell me they cannot meditate. This seems to me a bit like saying they cannot play the piano after one attempt. Meditation, as in every art or expression, requires constant practice for perfect results. A truly great pianist, for instance, would feel he could not play his best if he missed one day of practice. If he missed a week or a month of practice he would know that even his most uninitiated audience would recognize his defects. So it is with meditation. If we practice daily with joy in this daily habit, we perfect it as an art. I find that those who complain of the difficulty in meditation do not make it a daily practice, but rather, wait until something pressing appears in their world and then, through an act of will, try to fix their attention on the desired state. But they do not know that meditation is the education of the will, for when will and imagination are in conflict, imagination invariably wins.

The dictionaries define meditation as fixing one's attention upon; as planning in the mind; as devising and looking forward; engaging in continuous and contemplative thought. A lot of nonsense has been written about meditation. Most books on the subject get the reader nowhere, for they do not explain the process of meditation. All that meditation amounts to is a controlled imagination and a well sustained attention. Simply hold the attention on a certain idea until it fills the mind and crowds all other ideas out of consciousness.

The power of attention shows itself the sure guarantee of an inner force. We must concentrate on the idea to be realized, without permitting any distraction. This is the great secret of action. Should the attention wander, bring it back to the idea you wish to realize and do so again and again, until the attention becomes immobilized and undergoes an effortless fixation upon the idea presented to it. The idea must hold the attention – must fascinate it – so to speak. All meditation ends at last with the thinker, and he finds he is what he, himself, has conceived.

The undisciplined man's attention is the servant of his vision rather than its master. It is captured by the pressing rather than the important. In the act of meditation, as in the act of adoration, silence is our highest praise. Let us keep our silent sanctuaries, for in them the eternal perspectives are preserved.

Day by day, week by week, year by year, at times where none through love or lesser intentions were allowed to interfere, I set myself to attain mastery over my attention and imagination. I sought out ways to make more securely my own, those magical lights that dawned and faded within me. I wished to evoke them at will and to be the master of my vision. I would strive to hold my attention on the activities of the day in unwavering concentration so that, not for one moment, would the concentration slacken. This is an exercise – a training for higher adventures of the soul. It is no light labor. The ploughman's labor, working in the fields is easier by far.

Empires do not send legions so swiftly to obstruct revolt as all that is alive in us hurries along the nerve highways of the body to frustrate our meditative mood. The beautiful face of one we love glows before us to enchant us from our task. Old enmities and fears beleaguer us. If we are tempted down these vistas, we find, after an hour of musing, that we have been lured away. We have deserted our task and forgotten that fixity of attention we set out to achieve.

What man is there who has complete control of his imagination and attention? A controlled imagination and steadied attention, firmly and repeatedly focused on the idea to be realized, is the beginning of all magical operations. If he persists through weeks and months, sooner or later, through meditation, he creates in himself a center of power. He will enter a path all may travel but on which few do journey. It is a path within himself where the feet first falter in shadow and darkness, but which later is made brilliant by an inner light. There is no need for special gifts or genius. It is not bestowed on any individual but won by persistence and practice of meditation. If he persists, the dark caverns of his brain will grow luminous and he will set out day after day for the hour of meditation as if to keep an appointment with a lover. When it comes, he rises within himself as a diver, too long under water, rises to breathe the air and see the light. In this meditative mood he experiences in imagination what he would experience in reality had he realized his goal, that he may in time become transformed into the image of his imagined state.

The only test of religion worth making is whether it is trueborn; whether it springs from the deepest consciousness of the individual; whether it is the fruit of experience; or whether it is anything else whatever. I shall endeavor to show you that the methods of mental and spiritual knowledge are entirely different.

For we know a thing mentally by looking at it from the outside, by comparing it with other things, by analyzing and defining it; whereas we can know a thing spiritually only by becoming it. We must be the thing itself and not merely talk about it or look at it. We must be in love if we are to know what love is. We must be God-like if we are to know what God is. Meditation, like sleep, is an entrance into the subconscious. "When you pray, enter into your closet, and when you have shut your door, pray to your Father which is in secret and your Father which is in secret shall reward you openly."

Meditation is an illusion of sleep which diminishes the impression of the outer world and renders the mind more receptive to suggestion from within. The mind in meditation is in a state of relaxation akin to the feeling attained just before dropping off to sleep. This state is beautifully described by the poet, Keats, in his ODE TO A NIGHTINGALE. It is said that as the poet sat in the garden and listened to the nightingale, he fell into a state which he described as "A drowsy numbness pains my senses as though of hemlock I had drunk." Then after singing his ode to the nightingale, Keats asked himself this question, "Was it a vision or a waking dream?

Fled is the music; do I wake or sleep?" Those are the words of one who has seen something with such vividness or reality that he wonders whether the evidence of his physical eyes can now be believed. Any kind of meditation in which we withdraw into ourselves without making too much effort to think is an outcropping of the subconscious. Think of the subconscious as a tide which ebbs and flows. In sleep, it is a flood tide, while at moments of full wakefulness, the tide is at its lowest ebb. Between these two extremes are any number of intermediary levels. When we are drowsy, dreamy, lulled in gentle reverie, the tide is high. The more wakeful and alert we become, the lower the tide sinks. The highest tide compatible with the conscious direction of our thoughts occurs just before we fall asleep and just after we wake.

An easy way to create this passive state is to relax in a comfortable chair or on a bed. Close your eyes and imagine that you are sleepy, so sleepy, so very sleepy. Act precisely as though you were going to take a siesta. In so doing, you allow the subconscious tide to rise to sufficient height to make your particular assumption effective. When you first attempt this, you may find that all sorts of counter-thoughts try to distract you, but if you persist, you will achieve a passive state. When this passive state is reached, think only on "things of good report" -- imagine that you are now expressing your highest ideal, not how you will express it, but simply feel HERE AND NOW that you are the noble one you desire to be. You are it now.

Call your high ideal into being by imagining and feeling you are it now. I think all happiness depends on the energy to assume the feeling of the wish fulfilled, to assume the mask of some other more perfect life. If we cannot imagine ourselves different from what we are and try to assume that second more desirable self, we cannot impose a discipline upon ourselves though we may accept discipline from others. Meditation is an activity of the soul; it is an active virtue; and an active virtue, as distinguished from passive acceptance of a code is theatrical. It is dramatic; it is the wearing of a mask. As your goal is accepted, you become totally indifferent to possible failure, for acceptance of the end wills the means to the end.

When you emerge from the moment of meditation it is as though you were shown the happy end of a play in which you are the principal actor. Having witnessed the end in your meditation, regardless of any anti-climatic state you encounter, you remain calm and secure in the knowledge that the end has been perfectly defined. Creation is finished and what we call creativeness is really only a deeper receptiveness or keener susceptibility on our part, and this receptiveness is "Not by might, nor by power, but by my spirit, saith the Lord of Hosts."

Through meditation, we awaken within ourselves a center of light, which will be to us a pillar of cloud by day and a pillar of fire by night.

School of Life

Neville taught that the Bible is addressed to the imagination and God is within us as our wonderful human imagination, he insisted that God is not some being in the sky that we pray to, but that God is in us, that we are God and our imagination is the same power that created and sustains the universe. However as we are placed in the physical outer world, our imaginative acts take time and persistence to come into form. If we do persist in living in the feeling of the wish fulfilled, it will manifest.

He often quoted scripture and quotes from the Bible in an effort to explain the true meanings of the stories within the Bible. The stories within the Bible are addressed to the sleeping mind, in other words the subconscious mind. The God in mind, the human imagination. Our imagination knows no limitations, there is nothing that you cannot conceive of being or doing within the imagination. It is our outer self, our reasoning mind, the conscious mind, tied to the evidence of the senses, which imposes limitations upon what we believe we can do, be and have. We must go beyond this outer self, and live and feed upon our desires through our imagination and feeling, and ignore any evidence of the physical senses, which contradicts our desired state.

This world we are in is like a School, the school of life, just as we send our children to school to learn, so God in his love for us, sent us out to this School of life. So that we may remember who we are. So that we learn the joy of creation. We are not being punished, we are here to learn. Forgetting who we are, we make mistakes and we create undesirable states and suffering. We are still learning, but now knowing who we really are, and that imagination creates reality, we can set about changing these undesirable states. Through our imagination and feeling we can transform the undesirable to the desirable.

We create through faith, the belief that if we create an image in our imagination and assume the feeling that would be ours if our wish was a present fact and remain faithful to this unseen state, then what is not yet seen will become seen. We walk by faith in our imagination and not by sight.

You do not have to figure out how it will come about, or who will help you achieve your desire. You imagine the end and through your imagining clothed in feeling, and if you are persistent and remain faithful to it, the whole world if needed will be moved to aid you in the realization of your desire. This is what we are here to learn in this school of life.

Your imaginative acts, inner conversations and feelings go out of you and affect everything and everyone in your world. It has a ripple effect on your outer world and your world, forever your mirror will reflect back to you, in the form of, people, events and circumstances the results of your imagination and feelings. You cannot escape your inner conversations, imagination and feelings, as it is out pictured in your reality, to the minutest details in your daily life.

We are here to awaken and upon awakening we can begin to change our life. We no longer blame others or claim to be a victim of our circumstances. We arise, we look up and we assume the feeling that would be ours, if we were already the man or women we wish to become, and if we remain faithful to it, what we experienced in imagination will harden into fact and we will actually become it.

In the following lecture Neville explains this school of life in detail, and goes on to give you practical examples of how you can put your imagination to the test now. He describes spiritual sensation the inner senses of the imagination, and the creative power of these spiritual inner senses. Imagination creates reality, it's time to graduate in this great school of life and achieve your dreams.

That Which Already Has Been

Neville Goddard Lecture

This platform is concerned only with the great secret of life. Here we are convinced that the Supreme Power that created and sustains the universe is Divine Imagining, and it does not differ from human imagination save in degree of intensity. So God-in-man is your wonderful Imagination; that is God. We tell you that Imagination creates Reality, but bear in mind that at this human level on earth it takes time and persistence. If we will persist in the image, live in it, sleep in it, breathe in it, it will crystallize into tangible form.

Night after night we take different facets of this truly great secret, and as we turn to the greatest book on Imagination in the world, we treat it differently. So, as we turn to it, bear in mind that the Bible is addressed to the Imagination, not to the man of sense or the man of reason – the one that is "lost" or "dead" or "sound asleep."

We will take a simple little verse and show you why it is not addressed to the natural man, Ecclesiastes 3:15: "That which is, already has been; that which is to be, already has been; and God seeks what has been driven away." The "natural man" cannot grasp that, for to him reality is based only on the evidence of the senses. The man of reason could justify the verse's end, saying if it has any meaning then the writer must mean recurrence.

The sun comes every day and the moon completes its cycle and the seasons come and go. If we took a picture of the universe today, the scientists can compute how long it will take to return to this point in the picture. So the intellectual man could justify the verse; but that is not what is meant, for it is addressed not to the man of reason or the man of sense, but to the man of Imagination. What is it all about?

That which is, already has been; that which is to be, already has been, and God seeks what has been driven away." We are told that he made generic man (male-female) in his own image and called them "Man." Then we are told that this man was driven out, and the priesthoods tell us he was driven out because of some "original sin." I send my child to school to prepare her for living in the world, not to punish her, but to do it I must send her out. In Barbados we have a good school system, though not beyond high school, and when I was a boy there I would see these children arriving from the other islands at the beginning of the school year with their new clothes and their new books. They thought it was exciting, not knowing what it was all about. But then the time came for the parents to kiss them goodbye and leave them in this strange place, and many a child cried himself to sleep not just for a night but for the whole term, such was their homesickness and loneliness. But the parents did it in love and left them there. Many sent their children to England for still higher education at great sacrifice, and they could not afford to bring them home for vacations, so they had to wait years to see them again. But they did it in love and only love.

An infinite being of love did the same thing to us. We were "dead." We were fully made and perfect but we were like the statue of Galatea. And then to quicken man and make him like God, he had to drive him out – not in space, out in mind. So God became man, the thing that was dead, and to do it he had to lower himself to this level – which in comparison to the higher states would be called "dead." This garment of skin you wear has been long in preparation for the Son of God. We are told: "And He clothed them in garments of skin." It is for schooling purposes. Why are we here? To make images. The whole universe is an image of cosmic fancy.

We are learning, so we begin with the simplest things – a job, a new home, a change in environment. We do it in the same way as our Father did it, but this is a classroom so we make mistakes – but the fault is not ours for we are not yet awake. There was the perfect system, existing for its creator, and then God set free certain portions of it, and so he "prepared the way for his banished one to return." God seeks what has been driven away, so that he may say:

"This, my son, who was dead [and] is alive again." So we are the one he is seeking. There is something hidden in this coat of skin that he is seeking. We must get beyond the senses and begin to create.

So I say to everyone that we must start the art of creating, no matter how simple or how big the thing is, no matter what it is, that is creating. We create by faith, and faith is belief in the thing not yet seen. We create by assembling an image that implies we now have what we want in this world, and if we are faithful we bring it to pass, and as we do it we begin to move through this labyrinthine way for the return of his Son. "Whom God has afflicted He will comfort and call his friend." So if you are hurt do not believe that it was because of what you did in the past. No. We pass through the fixed labyrinthine ways that he has prepared for the return of his Son. So the Son finally awakens and he walks with me through the whole roadway of these states.

You can create anything in this world if you know who you are, and if you do not know, that is why these platforms exist to teach you, for we are all interlaced. You may think you are insignificant; you may even be in jail – but even behind bars you are creating. And you need not remain in jail if you know who you are.

Have you ever flown over a lake or over the ocean? A friend recently flew in from San Diego. He had been in the navy and he had always owned boats, but he had never before observed what he saw now from the air. He was on the ocean side as the plane took off from San Diego, and looking down he saw this little thirty-footer coming in the opposite direction. He noticed the wake of this little ship and watched it widen, and nothing interrupted it. When his plane turned inland he was flying at three hundred miles per hour, but looking back he realized that this little boat – doing maybe thirty knots – was troubling the entire Pacific. As far as the eye could see this wake was moving and nothing could stop it and the occupant of that boat was totally unaware of what he was doing. We are all like that. You think you can imagine and not affect others? It is like the wake: in time it encompasses the whole world. It starts as a little "v" but it grows wider and wider. Everyone will be in some way influenced by my pattern.

If one knows what he wants for himself or for others and remains faithful to it, he does not have to ask: "Who will help me?" For every person who must play a part will play it to make possible the fulfillment of that dream. A lady said to me the other night: "Look at my hands! A week ago they were blistered as if with acid; now there is no scar, but it took me five days of revision[1] to bring about what you are seeing." For unnumbered days prior to this nothing happened, but five days of revision brought this about. She produced in her own body this change. This seems stupidity to the rational man; to the Greek it is foolishness and to the Jew a stumbling block. It means that the man of reason cannot comprehend it; he cannot believe that one can create by imagination.

The way is prepared for you, for there are unnumbered states, and we can create states to deliver others and pull them out of those into which they have fallen. We are here on the earth as in a great schoolroom. We were not sent here to be punished, but to learn to become creators like our Father. There is no "original sin" for God made the decision to send me to "school." In fact I was "dead." I existed only for God, the creator of the perfect system, and then came the decision to subject me to this schoolroom in the hope I would be set free in the glorious liberty of the sons of God. Given the choice, what child would go to school? But loving the child the parents subject it to that training. How many years are taken from children's lives and given to learning? It is the same with us, only it is a vaster school. So let no one tell you that you did anything wrong in being born.

---

[1] Revision is Neville's technique, which is to mentally change anything that you don't want and change it to the desirable. See my book Mastering Your Inner World Neville Goddard Explained for practical application.

These coats of skin were prepared for us, for they help man – the invisible reality – to become conscious. And then some certain teachers sent by God tell them of the only value in the world and that is to awake. But if in the awakening you want a better home, a finer job, better health, then try to create it. Failure does not matter; you are learning. If you persist you will win. You create by faith. By faith the worlds were made and sustained. Things that are made are made from things that do not appear.

So what would it be like if you were the man you want to be? See the world as you would like to see it. Let me define Imagination for you. It is spiritual sensation, but the word "spiritual" is to most of us something that is not practical – the incorporeal as opposed to the corporeal. But Imagination is the power to perceive what is absent from the senses. Take a rose – there is not one here – but right now could I sense it in any way? Smell it? Touch it? I can, though it is absent from the senses. That is Imagination. If Imagination creates reality, such perception of what is absent from the senses makes it so. We have unnumbered case histories to prove it. Imagination is the power to perceive what is absent from the senses, and if you persist, you go beyond the sense man and go beyond the rational man. "The natural man receives not the things of the spirit of God for they are foolishness unto him."

How can I discern my home spiritually? I cannot see it with my physical eye or touch it with my physical hands, but in Imagination I can do both. You may say: "I do not have a home." Well, you do the same thing with a home you do not yet own. Do it with funds you do not now possess. Nothing has quite the same smell as money, or the same sound. If it is money you want, use every sense to make it real. But do not say: "I perceive it because I know it is there." To exercise the Imagination you see something that is not yet there. Then we get beyond the natural man, like the lady who in five days brought about a complete transformation in her hands.

Everyone is here for image making and to learn lessons, and the being who sent you here came with you and he has never left you. He became you and lit you with himself. As he lit man he awoke through the passage prepared for him into this schoolroom called earth. And then as he is lifted up he is embraced and given the ring and the fatted calf. "For this is my son who was dead and now lives again." For the first state was death and then comes the quickening of this state. He was lost and now he is found again. "That which is already has been; that which is to be already has been, and God seeks that which was driven away." So he drives him out by taking him out of mind. He is seeking Jacob in the Old Testament, and in the New Testament, Jesus. For when he finds him, he is Jesus. As he finds him, his is the reality of being, which is Jesus. He will find him in every being in the world. When this begins to awaken in you, the old form cannot contain it any more than new wine can be contained in old bottles. You cannot take this new wine of truth and confine it to the old dogma – it will blow it apart. So it has to take a new form as the Spirit begins to awaken within one. So make your image and ask no one to help you, for like the wake of the ship it will change the whole world, if it is necessary to the fulfillment of your drama. "Everything in the Pacific had to encounter that wake; nothing could stop it." You are the ark of God and what you are imagining is influencing all the others who are also imagining.

So Imagination changes things. Do not base it on facts. Truth as we see it is not confined to facts but depends only upon the intensity of Imagination. Everyone can do it – but often reason will interfere. A friend told me tonight that he desired the answer to a certain problem and it was given to him. He said: "I prayed to the being within me." It was a financial picture and he got the answer, but it seemed so stupid he did not apply it. Although he did share in it, it brought about everything that he desired. Reason interfered and he did not put his money into a certain venture. Reason stands between the man of sense and the man of Imagination.

Have you read Prodigal Genius, the Life of Nikola Tesla? He said there was nothing that was not within the Imagination. He conceived of alternating current, and when Edison told him it could not be done he said: "But I see it, and I am stopping it and starting it." And when they brought his model into the factory they did not change a bolt of it. A friend of mine, a violinist, cut an accurate model of something he had seen in his mind. It was a collapsible box such as now used by department stores to hold dresses and such. He had it patented and sold his patent for $10,000. Not one person in this country but has used that kind of box. Harry Webb got it in a vision. The manufacturer made millions. Harry did not labor for it. Reason was suspended and this came through.

Apply this principle to the little things of life and let no one tell you it is too material; the same ones will ask you for whatever it is when you discard it. You are here in this schoolroom to create out of your imagination and to do it by faith. Imagine and create the noblest concepts for yourself or for others and live in [them], and in a way you do not know, you will influence the lives of everyone in the world, and everyone who will be needed to bring about your dream will be drawn into it and brought to you. Even those who seek to stack the cards against you and think they are doing so very cleverly will find that the very thing they did will instead stack the cards against themselves. You are influencing everyone in this world when you are imagining. Who knows what being now in solitary is not disturbing the whole vast world. He will never be accused, for he is not out. They can find approximate cause, but they cannot blame him for he was in a cell. Yet he could cause a wave of hate out of the depth of his own being. That is why it is so important to imagine wisely.

There is only one being awakening and that is God, and we were put into this schoolroom in love even though many a night, like the children, we cry. Loving fathers here have sent their unwilling children to school; a loving heavenly father sent you here on earth. You apply it and use the greatest talent in the world, which is himself. That is Imagination. I cannot begin to tell you the thrill that is in store for you as you begin to live by Imagination. And then you can pass through all these states which were prepared for the return of his banished ones. Not a state but has been fixed before he put his Son into the depth to rise. So as he is the life of man, it is really God who is rising. So we deliver ourselves from states and at the same time deliver others from the same state. No matter what a man has done, he is only in a state and can be lifted out.

When we begin to awaken we will begin to comfort and heal, for whom God afflicts he did it for a sound end, and that was that he might awaken. "This is my son who was dead and now liveth." The most monstrous beast that ever walked the earth cannot be lost, for God is also present in him. If one could be lost then God could be lost, for he became his Son that he might awaken that Son as God.

So make your dream and live in it and it will come true. We are told that as the sower sowed, the seed fell on four kinds of soil. The first is not prepared; it is the highway, and no seed took root. These are those who will not listen. Then you will find one who will take this teaching, but it falls on stony ground. They get something new but there is no root. The first thing they say is: "Oh, it would have happened anyway!" The third fell among the "thorns and thistles." It grows deeper than the one on the rock, but they really believe that it is only with money they can get things and so the teaching was choked by the thorns of their unbelief. Then there is the well prepared ground, and it roots deeply and produces fifty and a hundredfold.

This ground has been prepared for your education and that it is all interwoven in the labyrinthine ways of your own mind. And then you learn to walk in the feeling of your wish fulfilled, and you can create states from this heavenly alphabet of God, and then we find how the entire Bible story is a true story as seen through the eyes of those who wrote it. It is the history of the soul of man and some day you will know it is taking place in you, and then it moves rapidly and you will understand the vision you did not understand before. Then you can say: "The whole Book spoke of me!"

So, speaking of the one that God is seeking, the one who was lost, who found him? God found him. You find it unfolding within you. And then you see that you cannot from now on use the old bottle or the old frame, for the vision differs and you cannot put new cloth on old garments, or new wine in old bottles, [and] your friends tell you that if you do this you will have no listeners. But you must go blindly on, because you have been given the new wine. You see no one who is important and you do not consider the wise or the foolish to be in supreme states, but you see them passing through these states into which we may all fall as we are being educated, as we move from the state of death to the divine liberty of the sons of God.

So if you get a vision, do not let reason interfere like my friend who lost $50,000 because he allowed reason to interfere and did not follow through on the answer that was given him. Reason divides the natural man of sense from the man of Imagination. Blake says: "Those who restrain desire do so because theirs is weak enough to be restrained, and the restrainer or reason usurps its place and governs the unwilling. And being restrained, it by degrees becomes passive, till it is only the shadow of desire." If you desire the recovery of a friend, do not restrain it, for then reason will restrain it. Let no one tell you he is suffering because of the past. You are called on only to forgive him. You are not the judge. Let no one tell you that your father punishes. He seems to do it for a purpose: "I kill, I heal, I wound, I make alive," etc.

Choose life, but there must be the contrary to awaken you. But we may choose from the tree of life, which is truth and error. So deliver anyone from the state into which he has fallen. [Now] you see what the prophet meant: "That which is already has been," etc., for the schoolroom is prepared for the awakening Son of God.

The Second Man

The second man whom Neville speaks about is your imagination, your power within, God in Mind, is sleeping until you become aware that your imagination is God, then you will experience the power of your imagination and ultimately you will have experienced God.

The First man is your conscious mind, the reasoning man, tied to the evidence of the physical senses; he feeds upon the facts of life, the objective world. The second man, your imagination, can feed upon any state; this is your subjective world, the world that is experienced in your imagination. And if you can detach yourself from your objective world and go within and feed your subjective world, that is your imagination (the second man), and feed upon this desired subjective state, with feeling. The second man (imagination), in time, will bring the subjective state, into form to the first man. That is the subjective state will harden into fact.

The Bible urges you to awake, to awaken to the knowledge that God is within you, that you are God. Your imagination is God and as nothing is impossible to God, nothing is impossible to you, if you believe it. In your imagination you prepare a state, which is you imagine you are the person you want to be, that it is already a present fact. You imagine the end and you feed that image with feeling and faith that it is done. Your imaginative acts go out of you, and then they will come again, that in time you will meet with them as events and circumstances. There is a time lag, but if you go within and prepare the state, and feed upon that state, you will receive it. Your hunger will be satisfied.

This is what prayer is. Prayer is nothing more than the feeling that your wish is fulfilled. The reason so many prayers remain unanswered is in the application. You don't beg and plead to a being outside of you in prayer, hoping that you are worthy enough to receive your request. Correct prayer is using your imagination and feeling to capture the mood that would be yours if your desire were realized, and remain faithful to the feeling.

All day long you are communing with self you are therefore in constant communion with God. Communion is defined in the dictionary as; the sharing or exchanging of intimate thoughts and feelings, especially on a mental or spiritual level. So your inner conversations, your reactions to life, your feelings, your thoughts, your beliefs, your daily mood, this is all in your imagination. You are in a constant communion with God continually all day, every day.

Look around you, what do you see? What is the state of your relationships? What are your finances like? What are the events and dramas in your life like? Is there a recurring theme of events in your life? Now look at your daily thoughts, feelings and reactions to life. Everything that has happened and is happening is a result of your use of your imagination, there is no escaping it.

Think of it this way, you are continually praying, the question is, what are you praying for? If you are allowing your imagination, your thoughts and feelings to feed upon the outer objective "facts", you are praying for more of the same. If however you learn to ignore the evidence of the senses, the outer man, and use your imagination to feed upon the thoughts, images and feelings of your desires, you are praying for and manifesting your dreams. There is no one to blame but self, everything that you are experiencing in your world, is created by you.

So what do you want? What is your desire? Single it out and go within, feed your imagination with the images and feeling of your fulfilled desire, appropriate the state, feed your subjective state, become absorbed in it, so that it crowds out all other ideas. Then continue to walk in that state in your daily life. Watch your reactions to life and you will know if you are being faithful to your desired state.

This next lecture from Neville, is all about capturing the mood, identifying the desired state and he talks about the first man and the second man. There are many practical examples of how to capture the mood, including a personal story of his.

Practice capturing the mood; learn to feed your subjective state, so that you may appease your hunger.

Catch the Mood

Neville Goddard Lecture

You will find tonight's message a very practical one. I don't think it will disturb anyone, but there are adjustments to be made concerning what man believes God to be, and what God really is. We are told in Scripture, in the birth of the twins, which begins the great drama as told in Scripture, "In your limbs..." and I am speaking now, not of anyone, but of you individually: "In your limbs lie nations twain, rival races from their birth; one the mastery will gain, the younger o'er the elder reign." (Genesis 25:23, Moffatt translation) These are in you individually.

We are told that the younger, which naturally is the second – the "second man" – is the Lord from Heaven. That's the Second Man; He sleeps in you. You will rouse Him, and He will become the Master. He will reign. At the moment, in the majority of the world, they are totally unaware of it. So, He sleeps, and so He doesn't reign. That one known in Scripture is called Jesus Christ; The Lord Jesus Christ is your own wonderful human imagination. That is God!

Now, the whole vast world, and all within it, is nothing more than the appeasement of hunger. That's the whole of life: the appeasement of hunger. And there are infinite states from which the Lord may view the world to appease that hunger. The "first man" can't do it. He can only feed upon what his senses dictate. Wherever he is, he feeds upon the facts of life as he sees the facts. It takes the "Second Man" to disengage Himself from that restriction and enter into a state – any state in the world – and feed upon it, and then – in time – bring the "first man" to feed upon it.

We are told in the 14th chapter of John: "Let not your heart be troubled, neither be afraid. Ye believe in God, Believe in me also." (John 14:1) Now, this is not a man talking to you from the outside. "Believe also in me." "You believe in God, believe also in me." In the same chapter He is going to tell you He is God! But what man would actually believe that this Presence within himself is God? Now, He tells you: "Be still and know that I am God." (Psalm 46:10) This is not another man speaking to you, other than yourself, "Be still, and know that 'I Am' is God." Can you believe that?

If you can believe that, then all things are possible to you. For, "all things are possible to God." (Matthew 19:26) Can a man really believe that? That's what I am told in the 46th Psalm, "Be still, and know that – I...". Put the little word is in there now. Now we are told, He sleeps, and then came the call, "Rouse thyself. Why sleepest thou, O Lord? Do not cast us off forever." (Psalm 44:23)

This one sleeps in man. Man has to rouse Him. He doesn't know that his own wonderful human imagination is God! Now, "In my Father's house are many mansions. Were it not so, would I have told you that I go to prepare a place for you? When I go I will come again, and I will receive you to myself, that where I am, there ye may be also." (John 14:2, 3) Now, this conversation takes place in you individually, between the two. I am speaking now to my self, "In my Father's house" – I am the Father "...are unnumbered mansions" – states of consciousness. "Were it not so, would I have told you that I go to prepare a place for you? And when I go, I will come again, and I will receive you to myself, that where I am there ye may be also." I am standing here, and my senses tie me here in this room but I don't want to be here. I want to be elsewhere. I know my bank balance. I know my obligations to life. I'm tied by what I know.

The "outer man" feeds upon that, but he wants more than that. There is something in me – the "Second Man" who is born from Heaven – who is telling me there are "unnumbered mansions" into which I can go – you can't go – I can go and prepare it for you. But, "when I go to prepare it for you, I will come again and receive you to myself, that where I am, there ye shall be also." Now, how do I do it? I take a look at my world, and I am very restricted. Everything about me is something I would like to break through – transcend it, become a bigger person, a more secure person, where I'm doing a greater job in the world. All these things I would like to do but reason tells me I am not doing it, and my senses confirm my reason.

Now, is there something in me that is my True Self that can do it? Yes, my imagination can do it. In my imagination, I go and prepare the state. I actually go into the state and fill that state with my own being, and view the world from that state. I don't think of it; I think from it. When I think from it, I'm actually preparing that state. Then I return to where I left this – "the outer man," and once more fuse with it, and we become one, once again. Now I take him across a bridge of incidents – some series of events – that takes me towards the thing that I've prepared, and I take him with me and enter into the very state itself. He feeds now, literally, upon that state.

This is what I call prayer. I don't vote for it; I don't petition, I ask no being in the world – no one, including what the world would say is God. For, when you find God by being still, and know that "I Am" is God, then to whom can you turn for anything in this world, if you really believe Scripture, "Be still and know that I am God"? (Psalm 46:10) If you are not familiar with Scripture, read it in the 46th chapter of the Psalms of David, the 10th verse "Be still, and know that I am God," – then, to whom could you turn? It's an inner communion with Self. But man talks to an outside god and pleads with an outside god, and begs an outside god.

This reminds me of a dinner party that William Lyons Phelps gave. If you do not know who he is – in fact, who he was, he was one of the truly great educators in our country in this twentieth century: William Lyons Phelps. He and Mrs. Phelps entertained Edna Ferber, the writer. As they sat down to dinner, Mrs. Phelps said to him, "William, will you please say grace." He closed his eyes, bent his head, and after maybe ten or fifteen seconds he said, "Amen." And she said to him, "Why, William, I did not hear one word that you said"; and he said to her, "I was not talking to you, my Dear..." People sit down to say grace as: "Bless the hands that prepared this food," all these words meaning nothing. You go within, and you don't petition: you appropriate.

Prayer is nothing more than the subjective appropriation of the objective hope. I hope for so-and-so; I want it as an objective fact. Now, I must go within and appropriate it subjectively. So, prayer is the subjective appropriation of the objective hope. That is what I call "faith in God," which is nothing more than faith in my Self, for the Self of man – the true identity of man – is God! That is the "Jesus Christ" of Scripture. "Do you not realize that Jesus Christ is in you? Test yourselves and see."

That is what we are told to do in Paul's second letter to the Corinthians. Read it in the 13th chapter, the 5th verse, of II Corinthians. "Examine yourselves, to see whether you are holding to the faith. Test yourselves. Do you not realize that Jesus Christ is in you?" (II Corinthians 13:5, Revised Standard Version) Well, if He is in me, then where will I go to meet Him? How will I address Him? He is in me. He is in my very Self. I simply commune with my Self.

There are unnumbered states in the world, so I single out the state that I want to express in this world, and I don't ask you or anyone else in the world if it is good for me. I don't consult anyone. Does it come within the frame of the Golden Rule? What I am now asking, would I ask it for another? Would I ask another, if what I am seeking now for another is something I would ask for myself? Well, the Golden Rule is: "Do unto others as you would have them do unto you." If you keep that in mind, you cannot go wrong.

What's wrong with asking for anything in this world for another that you would ask for yourself? Is there anything wrong in being secure? Nothing. Anything wrong in being clean and wholesome and decent? Anything wrong in being one who contributes to the world's good? What's wrong with that? Is there anything wrong in being happily married, proud of the girl who bears your name, or she proud of the man whose name she bears? What is wrong with that? Forget that.

The whole vast world is a field to reap. You don't pick out this woman or that woman. Pick out the state. I want to be blissfully happy, and if I were, how would I see the world? And how would the world see me? Well, shut out the world and go within and appropriate that state. And from within, you let your friends see you, as they would have to see you if what now you are assuming that you are is really true. That is why I have titled tonight's talk, "The Mood" – catching the mood. This whole thing is based upon that mood.

The 25th chapter of the book of Genesis: and she brought forth twins, for in her limbs were these rival races – rival races from their birth, called in Scripture "Esau" and "Jacob"; and you think they were two individuals who lived thousands of years ago. No, they are right here in everyone in this world! These are the eternal states of consciousness personified in Scripture as two little boys. Scripture is not secular history. It is salvation history. And, so, they did not live thousands of years ago; they live now in you, and you have to give birth to both of them. You have given birth to the first one. The first one is your "outer man," the man who is now a man of the senses – a man who is covered with hair, as we are told. Esau came out first, and he was covered with hair all over. Whether you be female or male, you are covered with hair all over. That is the external you, the man of the sense world. Then in comes the "Second Son," and he is the smoothest skin lad, called Jacob. The name "Jacob" means to supplant. He is going to supplant his brother; he is the second, but he will come first. The Second Man is the Lord from Heaven, and the Second Son is your own wonderful human imagination.

When you stir it and rouse it and make him come into being, you can do wonders in this world. Try it right now. You sit here in this room – I stand here; I could, in the twinkling of an eye, put myself outside of this room and view it from there, and see the interior of this room, not from this lectern, but see it from the outside. That is exercising the Inner Man. Go outside mentally, not physically, and view this room from the outside. While seated here, I can put myself in my hotel room downstairs, and then view this room and think of it, but thinking from my room downstairs. I can put myself in any part of the world and think from it, and think of the world and everything else.

That is the secret: thinking from what I want, instead of thinking of what I want. When I know what I want in this world, when I am thinking of it, it is always beyond me. When I know what I want, I enter into that state and think from it. Put yourself mentally into your own home tonight now, and view this building – this club – from your home, and you see this building, not from it; you think of it, and you are viewing it from your room. Now, the state of consciousness to which you most constantly return is the place you really dwell – that habitual state from which you view the world. Do you view it from poverty, saying, "I am poor?" Do you walk the street feeling, "How poor I am?" You are then viewing the world from the state of poverty. Am I viewing the world from the state of one who is completely unknown and unwanted? Well, that's my home.

The place to which I habitually return constitutes my dwelling place. I need not dwell there. "In my Father's house are unnumbered mansions. Were it not so, would I have told you that I go to prepare a place for you?" And when I go and prepare the place, I will return again and take you with me, that where I am – in that state prepared – you shall be also. So, I now take a state. I want to be known. I want to contribute to the world's good. I want also to live well – and I mean well. I want to feel secure, not only financially, but secure socially, that when I enter a room I am not embarrassed, no matter who they are. They can have all the degrees in the world. They can come from all the great universities in the world and be honored by the world. But I want to stand in their presence and not feel little. I want to feel a man. I am not to bow my head in shame because of any restriction in my past. If I were born "behind the 8-ball" socially, financially, intellectually, it doesn't matter. I want to feel important; I want to feel great. I want to feel right.

All right, what state would that be if it were true? I conceive a state that, if it were true, that would make all my wishes come true. I go into that state. Now, the first time I enter the state and view the world from it, it is wonderful, but I may never re-enter that state. Therefore, it is not my home. I want to make that state my perpetual home, so I automatically dwell in that state, and if I dwell in it so that automatically I am in that state, it becomes my dwelling place. So, "I will go and prepare a place for you." I am not talking to you; I am talking to myself: "I will take you, Neville, born behind the 8-ball – born unknown, unwanted, poor – everything that is simply behind the 8-ball, and I am going to take you, Neville – now that you have found me, the Second Man, the Lord from Heaven, your own wonderful human imagination – now that you rouse me, I will go." And I will dwell in the state and feel myself to be Neville – that "outer man" I just left on the chair or left on the bed, and I will see the world as Neville would see it if he were with me now. I view the world from that state. And, then, when it seems natural to me, I return to the physical "outer man" that I left on a chair – that I left on the bed and as I return, we fuse and become one person, not two.

Then I move across a bridge of incidents that I don't really, rationally build – it simply appears, and I move across a series of events that I do not reasonably determine – they simply happen. I will move across this bridge of events up to the state where I entered and now dwell. But when I get there, it seems so natural! The man that thought, because of his past limitations, he could never enter that state – now he finds himself in that state. No matter whom he meets, he meets them from that state, and it is perfectly natural to him. This is the story that Scripture teaches to you, to me, and to every one in the world. But until you find God, which is your own Self, you aren't going to do it. "Be still, and know that 'I Am' Is God." There is no other God! And you think that's blasphemy? All right, the one who teaches the story was also accused of blasphemy, for he said, "I am God," and they picked up stones to stone him. It doesn't mean a man is making a bold statement on the outside. The "outer man" takes the facts of life – these are the "stones" – to stone him, and then he quotes Scripture, and he quotes the 82nd Psalm: "Is it not written in your scripture that I say, 'Ye are gods, all of you sons of the Most High'? If, then, I say that I am the Son of God, and the Son of God and God are one and the same Being, why do you stone me when scripture teaches you, you are the sons of God?" (See John 10:34-37)

So they could not stone him then because he was only quoting their book. Well, I am only quoting tonight your book, which is my book. It's the book to set every man in this world free if you know Who-You-Are. Your true identity is Jesus Christ! And Jesus Christ is not a being who came two thousand years ago and then departed. He said, "I am with you always, even unto the very ends of time." (Matthew 28:20) If He is with me always, where is He? He said, "I am with you always, to the very ends of time." Then where is He? I surely know where He is. The conversation now – I am quoting from the 8th chapter of the book of John. It is taking place in you. No one else is hearing it. I am only now quoting from a passage from the 8th [chapter] of John, "You are from below, I am from above; you are of this world, I am not of this world. I say you will die in your sins, for you will die in your sins unless you believe that I am He." (John 8:23, 24)

I am only quoting from the 8th chapter of the Gospel of John. In Scripture, above and within are the same; below and without are the same. So, when you read, "I am from above," he's telling you, "I am from within", for he tells you, "The kingdom of heaven is within you." (Luke 17:21) So, I am from above, therefore I am from within. You, the 'outer man' – you are from without, therefore you are from below. You are of this world. I don't have to remain anchored to what my senses dictate and tell me that I am. I need not be here. You, looking at me from the outside, as the "outer man," will say, "Neville is on the platform." Knowing my complete outer world, you would know my restrictions, my limitations. You do not know my ambitions, my dreams, my wishes. I, and I alone, know my ambitions and my wishes. The "Inner Man" knows them, and He knows how to enter these states and prepare a state for the "outer man" to fulfill it. The "outer man" can't do it. The "outer man" is completely anchored by his senses and confirmed by his reason.

Now, let me share with you a simple story. At the time that it happened, it seemed an impossible thing. Right after the war was over; I took the first trip out with my wife and little girl to the Island of Barbados in the West Indies. I made no preparation for return. I sailed from New York. I thought I would go and stay a few months in the island with my family, who were all in Barbados, making no preparation for my return. Then it came time for my return, for I had a schedule in New York in the first week of May. I arrived in Barbados the last of December and had these four heavenly months – or almost four. When I went to the steamship company, they showed me a list which was as long as from here to there [indicating] of people waiting to get on the boat. That was only in the Island of Barbados. There were lists equally long in all the other islands: Trinidad, St. Vincent, Grenada – all the islands, and only two ships servicing all the islands: one little one taking sixty passengers, and one taking a hundred and twenty-five passengers; and hundreds and hundreds in each island waiting.

Well, they said, "Why, Mr. Goddard, you couldn't get out of this island until the month of October at the earliest." I said, "Is that your final verdict?" They said, "Why, that's final. Look at the list, and this is only in Barbados." This is the month, now, of April. I never thought of applying before that. My brother Victor said, "How on earth could you have left New York, the capitol of the world – the financial capitol of the world – they know everything there how to do these things. Why didn't you arrange there when you left for return?" I said, "It never occurred to me. It doesn't really matter."

I sat in my hotel room in Barbados and got comfortable, and then I assumed that I was in a little boat – a little tender, taking me off to the waiting ship in the bay. I could feel the rock of the little boat. In that boat I placed my family – a few members of my family: my brother Victor, my sister Daphne, and one or two others, and naturally my wife and my little girl. Then I felt the ship come alongside the main ship that would take us back to New York. And, then, in my imagination I assumed that my brother Victor took my little girl and stepped on the gangplank and walked up with her and I aided my wife next, and then my sister Daphne, and then I got on, and we went up. When I got to the top of the gangplank – all in my imagination, giving it all the sensory vividness, giving it all the tones of reality – I have no committed stateroom, so I could not go down to the stateroom. I simply turned at the top of the gangplank, walked three or four steps, and then put my hands on the rail, so I could smell the rawness of the sea, I could feel the salt driven by the wind. I could feel it on the rail, and then I looked towards the island with nostalgia. I was leaving a perfectly lovely island with so many members of my family, and yet it was a divided feeling. I was happy to be leaving because I had to get back to New York on my way to Milwaukee, and then, at the same time, I was split in my emotion because there was a sadness – like a sweet sadness leaving them and still happy to go. And that's the mood that I caught. I caught that feeling. I can't tell you if you haven't had the experience of going any place being divided between wanting to go and yet reluctantly so, because you are leaving something precious behind you. Well, that was my mood. I caught the mood. And then I kept on looking at the island, and then I broke it and here I am, sitting in my chair in the room in the hotel in Barbados!

The next morning the phone rang. As I answered, it was the Alcoa Steamship Company calling: "Mr. Goddard, we've just received a cable from New York canceling a passage sailing on the next ship, which could put you in New York on the first day of May. Would you like it for you, your wife and your daughter? It's a smaller stateroom, really, there are only two bunks, but your little girl is only three years old, and so she could sleep either with you or with Mrs. Goddard, but there are two bunks, and there is a private bath. Everything is perfect but you know; the ship is small. It will only carry sixty passengers." I said, "I'll be right down."

So, I went down, and I thought I would find out some more details. I asked the agent, "Why the cancellation?" "Well," she said, "I could only speculate. They didn't tell us: they cabled us. There was a cancellation for the return trip." I said, "All right, it's canceled. Why didn't you give it to any of the others waiting?" There were hundreds and hundreds waiting. "Well," she said, "we have one lady here – an American lady who has been bothering us week after week to get her out of Barbados back to New York, so we called her first, and she said, 'It's not convenient for me to go now.'

So, then we called you because you have three to go, and I thought you could use the room for the three of you. And we will not notify any of the other hundreds waiting." So, I asked no further questions. I took it and got back in time for my place in New York and then my place in Milwaukee.

When I first tell that story, the usual reaction is: Was that a fair thing to do? Can you imagine that! Was that a fair thing to do with all the others who were waiting? I wasn't running the Alcoa Steamship Company. I was applying the principle of God. I wouldn't care if one million people were there; I'd jump over one million. That's not my concern. I am simply applying the Law of God: "When you desire, believe that you have received it, and you will," as I am told in the 11th chapter of the book of Mark, 29th verse, and whatever you do, whatever you say, if you do not doubt that it will come to pass, it will be done for you. Well, I did what I'm told in Scripture I ought to do, believe that I had received it, and act upon that belief.

So, I acted upon the belief. What would I do if it were true? I would go up the gangplank. In those days, back in 1945, we did not have a deep-water harbor; we have one now. But then you had to go out to the ship by a little tender, so I did exactly what I would have to do if I went aboard the ship. So, I got aboard the little ship, and then, as we got to the big ship, strangely enough, my brother Victor went up with my little girl in his arms – the very first one to step off. And then here came my wife, here came my sister, just in the order that I had imagined it. I wouldn't care if that order was broken or not, but it did happen in the order that I imagined it. So, I tell you, I have found Him. Who? Found who? I have found the Lord Jesus Christ. You did? What does he look like? He looks just like me! Have you found Him? Well, don't look at me, because when you find Him, He's going to look just like you! That's the Lord Jesus Christ – just like you. There is no other Lord Jesus Christ. He actually became you that you may become the Lord Jesus Christ. And when you see Him, He is just like you.

So, do not turn to anyone in this world and say, "There he is," for that's a lie, or, "Here he is" – that's a lie. So, anyone telling you that Neville is the Lord Jesus Christ – your Jesus Christ, deny it! Deny it completely. Neville is not the Lord Jesus Christ for you. But I have found the Lord Jesus Christ in me as my own wonderful human imagination. And I share with you what I have found. One day you will find Him as your own wonderful human imagination. Then will come the day that everything said of the Lord Jesus Christ in Scripture, you are going to experience in the first-person, singular, present-tense experience – everything said about him. Then you will know who the Lord Jesus Christ is. Then you will know who the Father is, who – really – God is!

Meanwhile, test him. Go to the extreme test. I tell you, you will find Him never failing. He's your own wonderful human imagination.

Well, in this story that we started tonight, the two sons are brought now to the father. The father is Isaac, and Isaac is blind. There were two sons; the first one is Esau. He is covered with hair. That's every child born of woman; that is the "outer man," for hair means the most external, objective thing in the world. In man, the hair comes first, then you get the skin, then you get the fat, then you get the bones, but the hair is the most external part of man. So, he is covered with hair. The next one has no hair. He is hairless. He is Jacob, The word means supplanter. The father has requested a meal. That is why I told you earlier the whole vast world – the whole of life is nothing more than the appeasement of hunger.

So, the father is hungry, and he wants venison properly prepared as he always loves it and he gives that command to his first son, Esau. Esau was a hunter. He goes hunting for the venison, and prepares it to please his father. Jacob overhears the request of his father. Remember, his name is supplanter but the command was given to his brother Esau, So, he slays a goat and skins it, and puts the skin upon his body to deceive his father into believing that he is Esau. He prepares the goat and brings it to his father, and he says,

"Father," and Isaac answers, "Yes, my son." Then Isaac said, "I am blind, my son. I cannot see. Come close that I may feel you, that I may touch you." And covered with the skin of the goat, he comes close, and Isaac stretches forth his hand and touches him.

He said, "You know, your voice sounds like my son Jacob, but you feel like my son Esau," and then he gave him the blessing. And, then, having been given the blessing, Jacob disappears. Then his son Esau comes with the venison, and he said, "Who are you?" He said, "I am your son Esau." "Well," he said, "it must have been your brother who came, and I thought him to be you, and I gave him the blessing; and I cannot reverse it. I cannot take it back. I have blessed him, and the blessing remains his." So, you close your eyes, and you are Isaac; you cannot see. Isaac is blind. Shut your eyes, and you can't see the room. Now, inwardly you have the two sons. The outer room is your Esau. You shut it out completely, and they both go hunting. Esau comes after; Jacob comes first, and he gives the tones of reality to his father. His father is his own wonderful "I AM." Well, that's God! God's name forever is "I AM."

So, I AM is waiting to feel the tones of reality of what he wants, and he feels it to be so real, so natural. Now, he knows this thing is subjective, so he said, "You sound like Jacob, but come closer, my son, that I may feel you", and he feels him as I felt the rail on the ship, as I could smell the salt of the sea in the wind, as I could see mentally the island, as I could feel the ship rolling a little under my feet. All this was the tone of reality. This, now, is Esau; it seems real, and so I am giving a reality to this state – I am giving a blessing to it. Then I open my eyes to find I am sitting on a chair in my hotel room. Well, suddenly Esau returns. Well, Esau was the place that I left. The room that I sat in was my Esau; that was the objective world. It comes back. And I say, "What have I done?" I went into a state and I clothed it with reality. I gave it all the tones of an objective world, and it seemed so real to me that I gave it the blessing to be real – to be born.

Now this comes back, and without one word spoken, it is telling me, "You deceived yourself. You were deceived by my brother, the subjective state called Jacob." And I say to myself – knowing who God really is, He can't take back His blessing. He gave it the right to be born – the right to become objective – the right to become real, and in 24 hours it was born, – it was real. And, then, three weeks later I sailed on that ship and completed the entire journey. I've repeated it over and over again, and it never fails. And those who will believe it and who will put it to the test cannot fail. They cannot fail. This is the principle of Scripture.

So, will you actually give it the tones of reality? Will you actually, first of all, believe that the God that you now worship as something without, actually exists within you as your own wonderful human imagination? If you will believe that, and not think me blasphemous for telling it and think me something accursed for having spoken it – but may I tell you, I hope for your sake you will believe it. But really, in my heart of hearts, whether you believe it or not, I am not concerned, because the day will come you will have to believe it, because you will experience it. If only I can aid you to hasten the day – that's why I am here. But to actually say I am going to hit you over the head and make you believe it – no. I am not indifferent to your believing it; I can only appeal to you to believe it for your own good, that you may take whatever you have and transcend it by the use of this Law.

Whatever you have in this world, may I tell you, no one is really satisfied! I dined well today, but tomorrow I am going to be hungry. And hunger is forever with man, and God is the ultimate satisfaction of hunger, but that hasn't yet come upon the majority. He tells us in the 8th chapter, the 11th verse, of Amos: "I will send a famine upon the world; it will not be a hunger for bread, or a thirst for water, but for the hearing of the word of God." Now, that comes at the very end, for the average man is not hungry for the word of God. He is complacent. He will say, "I am a Christian!" So, what! "I am a Christian. I go to church. I contribute to the church," and so he thinks that means all that he does as a Christian – it stops right there. Well, the hunger is not satisfied, because when He sends that hunger upon the individual, nothing but an experience of God can satisfy that hunger.

Well, until He sends that hunger, all the other hungers can be satisfied, like the hunger for security, the hunger for a better job, the hunger for a raise in authority in your present position, the hunger for – you name it. Every hunger can be satisfied if you apply this principle. But then will come that day He will send the famine upon you, for you are the earth of which He speaks. It hasn't a thing to do with the world, the famine in the world, or whether there is famine all over the world, because they don't know how to satisfy their hunger. There is famine, but that is not the famine of which he speaks. He says it's not a hunger for bread; it's not a thirst for water, but for the hearing of the Word of God! So, I am giving you the Word of God as I personally have experienced it.

So, tonight you try it. Close your eyes to the obvious. That's Esau; send him hunting. And, then, become self-deceived. In his absence, bring in the "second son," who is the Lord from Heaven, and clothe him in the tones of reality, and feel how real it is. Give him all sensory vividness, and when it takes on the tones of reality, open your eyes! Then Esau comes back from the hunt, and then you tell him what you've done, and he cries out because your son – the "second man" – has deceived you and betrayed him the second time.

Every day you can apply this principle and become self-deceived, but it works. But always keep it within the frame of the Golden Rule, so that no one will be hurt. I do not care who did not get the passage north. I do not care what prompted the woman not to take it. I do not care what prompted the passenger from New York to cancel it. I have no complaints, no words; I simply did what I was called upon to do. I wanted to get out. I found myself locked in – locked in until October at the earliest, with my commitments in Milwaukee going. I couldn't do that. I had to get back, and get back, I did!

So, I tell you, this principle cannot fail you. But we are the operant power. And you do not get down on your knees and pray to an external god. Do exactly what the great William Lyons Phelps did, and say to the whole vast world, "I am not talking to you, my Dear," – I am communing with my Self. And if I give thanks for what has happened, I don't give it to you; I give it to the Being-within-me – constant praise for this miraculous power that is housed within me. And you walk in the consciousness of being constantly praiseful for this miraculous power that became you, that you may become It!

And that power is the Lord Jesus Christ who is in you, and there is no other.

So, when the whole vast world is looking for Him to come from without, as the great evangelist today has said, "It is imminent. He is on us. He is coming. I am here to greet Him." He will wait forever in vain. For when He comes, He is not coming from without. When He comes, He rises from within, and you are He! So, he's reaching millions of people, but he's in kindergarten. And what do you expect? He cannot give them more than milk. But in time, you have got to be weaned from milk, and take meat, and then the true meaning of the great mystery of the Christian faith.

So, the world has accepted it in a little story. All well and good, but don't forever and forever go on seeing only the little story. Learn to extract the meaning of the story, and hope it unfolds within you. Meanwhile, you apply what you have heard tonight, and before I leave the City at the end of next week, you should be able to tell me that what you tonight desire you have.

The Sesamum Was a Sesamum

Creation is finished, every state that could ever be, everything that could ever be is already completed there are infinite possibilities; all we are to do is to reap the harvest. It is our imagination, thought and feeling which calls forth our harvest, which is the events and circumstances in our life. Our seedtime is our moment of response, the movement within us and our imaginative acts, what we reap as our harvest is the result of this. The seasmum was a seasmum, the corn was a corn. You have planted the seed and it will grow and take form in your World. What seeds are you planting? What can you expect to see as your harvest? Upon what state are you feeding your imagination? Poverty or Wealth? Health or Illness? Love or Loneliness? Joy or Despair?

The trouble is when we meet our harvest, we do not recognize it. If we are plagued with misfortunate events and circumstances, we wonder why these things happen to us. We say, surely I haven't created this? I would never ask for this, I would never want this, how can you say I created this? We have forgotten our seedtime. That moment of response, those inner conversations, the images in our mind, this is the planting of the seed in our imagination.

To put it another way, imagine you went out and threw a boomerang, but then you forget you threw the boomerang, and then in a little while, all of a sudden out of nowhere, boom, this boomerang hits you on the head. You would say, where did that come from? I wasn't expecting this? I didn't ask for this? You have simply forgotten you threw that boomerang! So you don't expect it to come back to you, but a boomerang will always come back to you. Just as your responses to life and anything planted in your imagination with feeling will always come back to you, in the form of events and circumstances.

So what would you like to see as your harvest in your World? You can either choose to continue to react and feel the way you have always felt and continue to esperience the same results in your life, or you can choose to deliberately and consciously change your reactions and feelings to conform to how you would like things to be. You can make the choice now to purposely and persistently, feel yourself into your desired state and then live and act in that conviction. Then you are mastering your inner world and through imagination and feeling you are consciously creating and changing the circumstances of life. You affect life, rather than reflect it.

I urge you not to give up if you feel that your desires or the changes you are seeking in your circumstances don't happen overnight, or next week. If you are persistent the desires, the changes will come, remember there is a time lag. There is a seedtime, and just as a flower needs time to grow from the planting of a seed, so does your desire. It will come, your new harvest will objectivity itself, walk in faith and not by sight.

The last lecture in this book from Neville is Seedtime and Harvest. I have read and studied this lecture hundreds of times, it is pure gold. It really does increase your awareness, everything just seems to click into place and your understanding of the reasons behind why things are happening in your World hits you hard.

The good thing is that once you become aware of why these things are happening and the reasons behind your circumstances, you can change it. And as you learn how to change it and apply the principles and techniques you are in for a real treat. You will not be able to contain your joy, when you experience this amazing power, this awesome gift, of your wonderful human imagination.

Seedtime and Harvest

Neville Goddard Lecture

As you have been told, this morning's subject is Seedtime and Harvest. Although it bears the same title as my latest book, it is not to be found in that book, for that book is an attempt to interpret some of the more difficult passages of the Bible.

But this morning's subject "Seedtime and Harvest". I want to approach it differently. This statement is taken from the Book of Genesis, the 8th chapter of Genesis - it is a promise made to man that "while the earth remaineth, seedtime and harvest, hot and cold, summer and winter, day and night shall not cease." We are told that man was placed in a garden - the garden was completed - every tree was bearing fruit - everything in the world was finished - and he was placed in the garden to dress it and to keep it. He doesn't plant it, he doesn't do a thing but dress it and keep it. He is not called upon to make trees or to grow new trees - everything is finished!

As we are told in John - "I have sent you to reap that whereon you bestowed no labor"- for Creation is finished. Every conceivable human drama, every little plot, every little plan in the drama of life is already worked out, as mere possibilities while we are not in them, but they are overpoweringly real when we are in them.

So man can get in touch with that particular state of his choice, for my imagination can put me in touch inwardly with the state desired so I am in it. If I am in it I will realize it in my world. The states in which we find ourselves are the seed time. The harvest is simply the encountering of events and circumstances of life. But man's memory is so short he forgets the seedtime, but all ends run true to origins, so if the origin, say is misfortune the end will be misfortune.

But when you reap misfortune, you wonder "Why should it happen to me? When have I set a thing like this in motion? Haven't I given to the poor? Haven't I attended service? Haven't I prayed daily, and why should these things happen?" But you see my God never forgets because He always gives the end in harmony with the origin, and you and I are selectors: we don't make; we are not creators; - creation is finished, the whole vast world of creation, as told us in Ecclesiastes "I am the beginning and the end. There is nothing to come that has not been and is." So look upon creation as finished - and you and I are only selectors of that which is.

By selectors I mean that you and I have the privilege (we may not exercise it) but it is our privilege to select that aspect of reality to which we will respond, and in responding to it, we bring it into existence for ourselves. Not knowing that we are so privileged, we simply go through the world reflecting the circumstances of life, not realizing we have the power to create or to out-picture the circumstance of life.

So now let us now analyze what I personally mean by seedtime. If everything is finished and completed, then why the promise there shall be seedtime and harvest as long as the earth remains? Now seedtime, to those who are here this morning, as we should really know, we are not taking it literally, our seedtime is that moment in time when you and I react to anything in this world. It may be to an object, it may be to an individual, it may be to a bit of news that we have overheard, but the moment of reaction, that emotional response, is our attitude.

Our attitudes are the seedtimes of life, and although we may not remember the seedtime or the moment of response, nature never forgets, and when it suddenly appears in our world, that suddenness is only the emergence of a hidden continuity. It was continuous from the moment of reaction until it appeared in the world. Its appearance in the world is harvest so you and I may harvest anything we desire but we must first have a seedtime. It must be preceded by a moment of response or an attitude. How often you say, "I approached it in the wrong attitude" or "He is in the wrong attitude" or "You must change your attitude if you would get on in this life". I have said it - you have said it - maybe we have said it to each other - but we know the importance of right attitude.

We know this much: that I can change my attitude if circumstances change - that's automatic. We know that if something happens suddenly in my world of which up to that moment I was not aware, I, becoming aware of a change of circumstance would automatically produce in myself a change of attitude. We all do that, morning, noon and night, but that's not important, that is a reflect of life.

Ninety-nine percent of the world reflect life. Now, can I consciously, can I voluntarily, can I deliberately produce in myself a change of attitude, one of my own discretion, one that I myself single out, and not one that is determined by or in any way is dependent on a stimulus of a change in the object itself. Must you change before I will change my attitude towards you? We know that if you do change I will change my attitude towards you, but must I go through life simply reflecting these changes in the objects, and can I not deliberately determine the change prior to the change in the object?

For if I can, I am moving towards complete control of my fate and becoming the master of my fate if I can assume an active, positive attitude and not depend upon changes in the object for changes in myself. If I can do it, I really am, if not a complete master, I am becoming more in control of the circumstances of life, but ninety-nine percent of the world waits for things to happen on the outside and then they reflect; that's no accomplishment at all.

If we would awaken and become real selectors of the beauty of this garden that God gave us so that we can single out that particular aspect to which we will respond, then we will do it by deliberately changing our attitude towards life itself. There is a little fable given us to show us how it is done. If you will study the fable carefully, you will see the importance of imagination.

The fable is the fable of the fox and the grapes. You all know it. When he failed to obtain the grapes then he persuaded himself that the grapes were sour, and by imagining the grapes to be sour he evoked in himself a change of attitude. He no longer felt about the grapes as he formerly felt. Now that's a little fable on a negative tone or a tragic tone.

You and I take the same story but now we put it on a positive tone. We contemplate our ambitious dream, our noble concept of life. It may seem we haven't the talents to realize it - instead of saying what the fox did, that the thing is beyond us and therefore it is sour anyway, we can take the same technique and wonder what it would be like had we realized it. What would the feeling be like were we - (and we name it) - if I can contemplate what the feeling would be like were I the man that I want to be, were you the person that you want to be, and rejoice in that state as though it were true, I am producing in myself that emotional response necessary for seedtime. I may not see an immediate harvest, maybe the thing that I am now giving expression to in the form of seedtime is an oak, it is not a little mushroom that would grow overnight. Maybe my dream would take a little longer interval of time between the actual planting and the reaping, but if I know that all these things are consistent, - "See yonder fields! The sesamum was sesamum, the corn was corn. The Silence and the Darkness knew! So is a man's fate born" - so, if that moment of response is the actual planting of the seed, and if it was corn, it must be corn when it appears in harvest time, then I can select the nature of the things I want to encounter in my world.

I can take not just Neville as a man, I can take the request first of my circle, my intimate circle, as a family man - my wife's desires for her child, for her husband, for herself - the child's desire for itself - and move beyond my little circle as a family man into the circle of friendships, move beyond that into my acquaintances, move beyond that into total strangers, impersonal states, but if I know the law holds good, no matter when I operate it, if I do it unconsciously or consciously, you get results regardless, and the results are in harmony with the planting, with the actual seedtime.

Now what is now our seedtime today? There are maybe two thousand odd here, we have two thousand odd different requests, multiplied by a large number because we have requests for others but you can take, today, as you sit here and you can actually contemplate what it would be like - suppose it were true. Suppose I could turn now to a friend and rejoice with him because of his good fortune and actually carry on a mental conversation with him from the premise that he or she has already realized the dream. Now as I do it in my imagination I am setting up within myself a certain changed attitude in regard to that individual. I am producing within myself a certain positive, deliberate, emotional response, and that very moment that I do it, is seedtime. I will encounter that individual tomorrow or next week or next month and he will bear witness of that thing I plant now. He may be totally unaware that I planted it in this garden. I am not seeking his praise, I am not seeking credit - I am seeking results. If I see the man become the embodiment of the success I know that he desires and I desire for him, that's praise enough, that's payment enough. What more payment would anyone desire other than the results, for everything is a gift. Why should I be given more!

My Father gave me the garden - the whole thing is in complete and full bloom and gave me choice - the greatest gift of all, complete freedom of choice of the nature of the fruit I will reap in my world; but I cannot just barge into the garden and start picking fruit - there must be a seedtime, but I must always bear in mind I will reap that whereon I bestowed no labor. I don't labor to make it so, I simply plant it, for in that moment of response is contained all the plans, all the energy necessary to unfold that plan into a perfect wonderful objective fact which I will then harvest by becoming aware of it as an external reality, but I don't labor to make it so; I simply must know it is so.

So that is our privilege that is our choice. If you believe it, aren't you amazed at the kind of things that you planted, at the kind of seedtime that in our ignorance, in our sleep, we allowed to actually scatter in our world? You see some will say, "But why does God allow it?" You cannot conceive of an infinite God that is not infinite in every respect. If I was incapable, actually incapable of assuming, say, an unlovely state, I could not be my Father's son because my Father is infinite, and if He were actually incapable of assuming any state then He would not be God.

Everything is within me - but everything. You cannot conceive of something that I don't contain - the most horrible thing in the world were it not so I could not be infinite, and, therefore, not the son of my infinite Father. So God is infinite and gave us everything, but He gave us freedom of choice that we may become selective, discriminative and bring out everything that is beautiful out of that garden.

If I took the piano, the eighty-eight notes of the piano, if I could extract from that piano keyboard every discord, I would not have a piano keyboard. If I could strike a discord and because it frightens me or it disturbs me, the thing grates upon my nerves; if I could now extract the notes that produce the discord and then keep on extracting the notes that produce the discord, I would remove the eighty-eight notes - there would be no notes left on which I could play tomorrow's harmony. But let me leave the notes and learn the art of playing the piano so I can from the same eighty-eight notes bring out all the harmonies of the world.

The same thing is true of man. Instead of looking at someone and accepting as final the evidence of the senses; there is someone who brought out into his own world, say disease: he is trying to analyze it from the outside - when did I contract the bug, when did I come in close contact with someone who had the bug and they are taking me into the laboratory with my blood and try to find it there. You will never find it there, in spite of all the wisdom of man. You will find it only in the consciousness of the individual, who, at a moment now long forgotten, planted the thing he is now harvesting - and you are not going to find it in any external analysis at all because things seen were never made of things that do appear.

You are warned time and time again in all the books of the Bible, but especially in that 11th chapter of the Book of Hebrews, that "things seen were not made of things that do appear" but no man believes it. He insists on finding it in things seen, so he extracts my blood, he extracts a little piece of my skin, and he starts to make an analysis of that, and he will tell me yes, he has found it. It's in my blood. I am not denying he has found it in my blood, but why is it in my blood? It is in my blood or in my body, or in my world because at some point in time, I, exercising the right as a free child of God, singled out some unlovely state relative to another. It need not be to myself; it could be to another, wherein I rejoiced in the hurt of another; where my emotional response to the news I heard was "good" so, I set it in motion, but when it happened in my world, I did not think it was so good but it was my harvest - and all these things are the harvest of things you and I have planted; for all things run true to form.

Don't be surprised at the suddenness in our world - someone is ill - it is only sudden because we have forgotten, and man's memory is very, very short. You know that lovely little poem of George Meredith: Forgetful is green earth; The Gods alone Remember everlastingly; they strike remorselessly, and ever like for like. By their, great memories The Gods are known.

If man could only remember these moments of seedtime, he would never be surprised when the harvest appears in his world. But because he has no memory as to that moment in time when he dropped that seed, which is simply his emotional response to something he contemplated, something he overheard, something he observed, at that moment the thing was done; he didn't have to labor to bring it to harvest - he simply encountered it as something already full grown, so he reaps now that on which he bestowed no labor, outside of choice. He selected it by his attitude, by his reaction.

Now, am I responsible for others in my world? I certainly am! When I take my little mind, my little imagination and think because it's mine - my Father gave it to me, that I can simply misuse it, it isn't going to hurt another. I tell you, you do have to use more control for the simple reason I am rooted in you and you are rooted in everyone and all of us are rooted in God. There is no separate individual detached being in my Father's Kingdom. We are one. I am completely responsible for the use or misuse of my imagination.

Do you recall seeing on TV, a dramatized version of the sinking of the Titanic? Do you recall it? Have you read the book, "A Night to Remember"? Well the book itself is by Walter Lord: but 14 years before the actual harvest or that frightful event of the sinking of the Titanic a man in England wrote a book. He conceived this fabulous Atlantic liner and there he built her just like the Titanic, (only the Titanic was not built for 14 years) but he, in his imagination, conceived the liner of 800-ft. She was triple screw, she carried 3000 passengers, she carried few lifeboats because she was unsinkable; she could make 24 knots; and then one night he filled her to the brim with rich and complacent people, and on a cold winter night he sunk her on an iceberg in the Atlantic. 14 years later the White Star Line builds a ship. She is 800 ft., she is a triple screw, she can make 24 knots, she can carry 3000 passengers, she has not enough lifeboats for passengers but she, too, is labeled unsinkable. She is filled to capacity with the rich, if not complacent, but the rich, because her passenger list was worth in that day, when the dollar was one hundred cents, two hundred and fifty million dollars was the worth of the passenger list. Today it would be a billion dollars. All the wealth of Europe and the wealth of this country was sailing on that maiden voyage out of Southampton.

Five nights at sea in this wonderful glorious ship and she went down on a cold April night on an iceberg. Now that man wrote a book either to get something off his chest because he disliked the rich and the complacent, or he thought it might sell or he thought this is the means of bringing him a dollar as a writer. But, whatever was the motive behind his book which, by the way, he called "Futility" to show the utter futility of accumulated wealth, but the identical ship was built 14 years later and carried the same kind of a passenger list and went down in the same manner as the fictional ship. Is there any fiction? There is no fiction! Tomorrow's world is today's fiction. Today's world was yesteryear's fiction - the dreams of men of yesteryear.

Wouldn't it be wonderful if I could talk with someone across space and just use a wire? And I couldn't see that one: it would be a mile away beyond the range of my voice - then maybe five miles and maybe a thousand miles - fantastic dreams - then they came true. When they came true, suppose I could do it without the means of a wire. And it came true; suppose now I could do it not just in an audio sense but in a video sense. Suppose I could be seen? And that came true, but when they were conceived, they were all fictional, all unreal. There is nothing unreal, because God is infinite, and God has finished creation. You cannot conceive of something that your Father has not only done and conceived of it, it is worked out in detail, in all its ramifications. You and I are only becoming aware of increasing portions of that which already is. We are not making a thing - we are discovering God's wonderful world.

But now in this church - at least here it should be done, for this is a church of the mind: this is Science of Mind, where there is a science to planting and you do it in a certain scientific manner. You just don't walk the street and reflect; read the papers and reflect - you go out a more positive person than people who gather in similar areas, for the simple reason they go just to hear a service and to be told how bad the world is. You're not coming here to be told how bad the world is, for if you believe it is bad, there is something you must do about it because you have planted the world. You have your seedtime. So here people gather to be told how to operate this wonderful gift that the Father gave them.

There is this wonderful mind and imagination. So you are told to go out and be choosey in your selection; single out that aspect of reality to which you want to respond, success, health, dignity, nobility, something wonderful that you contribute to the good of the world. As you walk by you are contributing to society, you contribute to the community in which you live, not necessarily by giving dollars but you contribute by your wonderful seedtime. If, in your community, you see the need of maybe a church, you see the need of some wonderful school, you don't wait until people get together, you actually, in your mind's eye, contemplate the joy that is yours because of the wonderful school here for the children, a wonderful church here to lift man spiritually, and you wonder what it would be like were it true; - you feel the thrill of witnessing it within. That is seedtime. Then in a way that you do not know and you need not labor to produce, you will encounter that school and that church and these lovely things in your community.

So you plant the seed and let others, who think that they are bringing it into being, let them think so. You go about this world planting the good - that is why you are here. We are gathered here on Sunday mornings to discover more and more about this wonderful gift that God gave us, that we may single out all the lovely things in the world and bring them to birth in our world.

This morning you take not only yourself - start with self - then turn to a friend in your mind's eye, and congratulate him on his good fortune - congratulate him on his expansion in his world, and actually feel the thrill of such contact - at that moment of response that was a changed attitude in regard to that friend- at that moment you planted. Now, in a way you do not know and you need not know, that seed is going to go through its normal natural hidden passage and appear as a reality in your world. Then you will know the power latent within you and you will stop reflecting life and you become one what I call a true creator in the sense that-I mean creator - that you are creating by selecting wise, wise, lovely things in this world and giving them expression in this world of ours. So that's what I mean by seedtime and harvest; the importance of the right attitude: and you can do it, you need not wait for circumstances to change, you need not wait for the stimulus of a change in the object to produce in yourself the change of attitude. In your office, does the boss act in a rude way towards you? Well then what would it be like if he now saw in me the lady, the helpful person that I really am, or want to be. Suppose he saw in me someone he could praise for my work and raise me in the salary world, give me an increase in salary because of my added effort; suppose he could see that in me, well, contemplate the boss seeing that in you as though he saw it and rewarded you with an increase. That moment is the moment of planting. It may not come tonight, it may not even come this week in the paycheck, but it will come.

You simply keep on planting the lovely things; but if every day when you leave the office you say, "What a skinflint", and you go home and you discuss him with your mother or your husband or someone else, and they sympathize because they really believe you, for they are playing the same reflective, negative approach to life; but if as you ride home or walk home, you walk in the attitude that he had done it - he had increased your income, he had praised your work, and day after day, in spite of other things to the contrary, you persist in it, do you know he will do it? You will produce in him the change of heart because you first produced it in yourself, and he will see in you qualities that he cannot now see, and then your whole vast world begins to blossom - you do it in every sense of the word.

You know someone who is lonely - one who really should be happily married in this world. What would it be like if you were told, not by the individual necessarily, but by a third party of the good news concerning John, concerning Mary or someone else. Someone desirous of a lovely home and a gracious home. What would it be like? Don't be envious. Try to rejoice. Feel the joy that is theirs, and that moment is seedtime for them. They will harvest it - and that is our opportunity to go through the world planting and planting wisely. Unfortunately, too many of us in church movements - I don't think you will find it in this church - but too many of us in church movements have a very serious attitude towards life. And, of course, the basic attitude is the attitude towards life, not necessarily the individual attitude towards an object or towards an individual, but the attitude itself that the individual adopts through life, towards life, and they have a very serious one. Well, Orage very wisely and very humorously said the serious attitude is this, - they really believe that God has an enormous struggle against helpless odds, and he said that produces in the individual the emotion of "helping poor Father". They go to help poor Father who has created the world and gave it to his children.

Now he brought up another interesting point of the scientific attitude towards life. Having discovered the little molecule or the little atom and the wonderful construction, that is, theoretically - having discovered this wonderful orderly construction of the bricks that make up the world, their attitude is one of orderly insignificance because they believe the world is gradually burning itself out, so no matter how orderly it is, if they really believe the sun will eventually go out and the earth will consume all its resources, what other attitude could they adopt than all dressed up with nowhere to go, because if eventually it is all going to be in nothing anyway, no matter how orderly it is today, it could only be orderly insignificance, but I tell you, as one who has seen beyond the veil, there is no such thing as coming to an end. Life is forever and forever and forever - and forever you are moving up this everlasting pilgrimage revealing the infinite glories of your Father.

So go out wisely today - go out determined to become more selective, more discreet in your choice of ideas you will entertain and single out the idea that would bless an individual and produce in yourself the emotional response that you have witnessed that state in his world, and know at that moment of response, you planted for that individual, and he is rooted in you, there is no such thing as he will not be found in your world for he is rooted in you. Everyone is rooted in you - therefore you will not lose them. It is planted relative to that being and that being is going to harvest it, and you will know the harvest when it appears in his world. You simply plant and let the harvest take care of itself.

The World is Your Oyster

Here we come to the end of this book. So what are you going to do now? Are you going to apply this wonderful life changing knowledge, or are you going to continue your search and never experience the truth of who you really are?

I urge you to apply it, to honestly try it, test your imagination and experience the power within you. Find God in Mind, this brings your seeking to an end. God is in you, do you not find that incredibly empowering? Does it not fill your heart with joy?

The World is your oyster, you can be do and have anything you desire. I am not saying that you will never again experience anything that you don't like, the difference is you will change your reactions to it and know that you have the power to change it.

Some of my greatest achievements have come into being after what looked like tragedy or negative events, sometimes the bridge of incident that you are led across in order to get to the fulfilment of your desire seems negative. There is nothing negative in and of itself, it's our reactions to it that make it negative.

You can only see part of the picture at any time, you cannot see the plan in its entirely, that is only revealed at the end when you reach the fulfilment of your desire and then you can look back and you see how it all worked out, how everything fell into place, it was all worked out in intricate detail, you just couldn't see it.

Stay in the feeling of the wish fulfilled no matter what is going on around you; don't allow the evidence of the senses to pull you out of your state. Live and act from the feeling of the wish fulfilled. This is the formula for success.

Begin today and be persistent, never ever give up on your dreams.

Imagination creates reality and you are the operant power!

About Neville Goddard

Neville Lancelot Goddard was born on 19th February 1905 in St. Michael, Barbados in the British West Indies; he was the fourth child in a family of nine boys and one girl.

Neville left his home land to travel to the United States to study drama at age seventeen and became a dancer and toured with his dance company, in one such tour he travelled to England and became fascinated with metaphysics. Upon his return to the United States he gave up his dancing career in order to commit himself full time to the study of spiritual and mystical matters.

It was around this time that he was introduced to his mentor and teacher, Abdullah who taught him Hebrew, the Kabbalah and the hidden symbolic meaning of Scripture. It was through these teachings that Neville first learned the power of the imagination.

In the 1950's, Neville began giving a series of talks on television and radio, and for many years lectured on the subjects of The Law and The Promise to capacity audiences at the Wilshire Ebell Theatre in the 1960's and early 1970's.

Neville also wrote several books on the power of imagination, including Feeling Is the Secret, The Power of

Awareness, Your Faith Is Your Fortune, The Law and The Promise, and more.

Neville Goddard died at the age of 67 on October 1st, 1972; his teachings however will live forever.

About the Author Rita Faith

For many years Rita Faith has studied the principles of the power of the imagination and the Law of Attraction. Rita studied the works of many of the great teachers on metaphysics, scriptures and spiritual and mystical matters.

It was during these studies that Rita was first introduced to the works of Neville Goddard, and it was at last at this time that she truly began to experience the power of imagination.
Neville's principles broke apart the laws of the universe like no other, offering profound insight into the various ways the mind attracts and creates the reality we live in.

Rita found through experience that Neville Goddard's teaching were by far the most accurate and comprehensive teachings on the laws of consciousness.

Having applied these principles Rita achieved massive success. It is her desire that everyone also achieve this success.

Therefore you will find that Rita Faith's books are based on Neville's teaching but broken down in such a way so to give a clearer understanding for the reader in today's age

If you have any questions, feedback or comments for Rita please contact her using the following email address.

ritafaithauthor@gmail.com

"If I could define prayer for anyone and put it just as clearly as I could, I would simply say, "it is the feeling of the wish fulfilled." If you ask, "What do you mean by that?" I would say. "I would feel myself into the situation of the answered prayer and then I would live and act upon that conviction." I would try to sustain it without effort; that is, I would live and act as though it were already a present fact, knowing that as I walk in this fixed attitude my assumption will harden into fact." – Neville Goddard

Printed in Great Britain
by Amazon